I0473771

BUILDING WEALTH
WITH DIVIDEND STOCKS IN THE
NIGERIAN STOCK MARKET

DIVIDENDS - STOCKS SECRET WEAPON

ALEX UWAJEH

Legal Disclaimers

All contents copyright © 2012 by **Alex Uwajeh** and http://www.247BroadStreet.com. All rights reserved. No part of this document or accompanying files may be reproduced or transmitted in any form, electronic or otherwise, by any means without the prior written permission of the publisher.

This book is presented to you for informational purposes only and is not a substitution for any professional advice. The contents herein are based on the views and opinions of the author and all associated contributors.

While every effort has been made by the author and all associated contributors to present accurate and up to date information within this document, it is apparent technologies rapidly change. Therefore, the author and all associated contributors reserve the right to update the contents and information provided herein as these changes progress. The author and/or all associated contributors take no responsibility for any errors or omissions if such discrepancies exist within this document.

The author and all other contributors accept no responsibility for any consequential actions taken, whether monetary, legal, or otherwise, by any and all readers of the materials provided. It is the readers sole responsibility to seek professional advice before taking any action on their part.

Readers results will vary based on their skill level and individual perception of the contents herein, and thus no guarantees, monetarily or otherwise, can be made accurately. Therefore, no guarantees are made.

Discount available for bulk buying

email: sales@247broadstreet.com

Acknowledgements

I am deeply thankful to my wife, Sarah and children, Ikechukwu, Nneka and Isioma for their loving support.

Also I would like to thank Chief and Mrs Sebastian Adigwe for their never ending love through both good and challenging times.

As always, I want to thank God for His grace, wisdom and insight.

With Dividend Stocks In the Nigerian Stock Market

Table of Contents

Introduction

Finding ways to build wealth and create a solid stream of passive income can be difficult for many investors. Yet, with the right information – and the right market conditions – it can be quite easy to build a strong portfolio of high-yielding stocks that will continue to generate income for as long as you own them.

The key to developing this type of portfolio is to choose a market known for undervalued and over-performing stocks. When you've located a market just like this, you then build a carefully selected portfolio designed to build wealth via capital and reap the rewards from high-yielding dividend payments.

Far too many investors set their sights on investing in their own local stock markets, believing local shares of local companies may represent a certain level of security for them.

What these investors may be missing is a huge opportunity to reap massive profits and high yields in international stock markets that freely allow international investors to buy stocks and shares very easily.

You see, international investing can take on three separate levels of wealth creation that many investors don't always recognize:

1) Growth of stock values in a foreign region
2) Increased yields on dividend returns
3) Increase in capital value due to changing currency exchange rates.

This is where the Nigerian Stock Market enters the picture.

Compared to some of the enormously large stock markets around the world, such as the New York Stock Exchange, the Nigerian Stock Exchange is relatively small. Yet it has a market capitalization of approximately N15 trillion (Nigerian Naira, which is approximately $125 billion US dollars).

The vast majority of investors hold the view of stock market investing as buying in low and selling once the stock price has risen far enough to represent a profit. Essentially, this is called trading. While this tactic is ideal for building capital value, it may not offer a sustainable long-term strategy to build wealth and create a stream of passive income.

By comparison, investing relates more to buying into a particular market with the view to holding onto the investment long enough to see it return solid results. This may be in the form of capital growth, but it can also be in the form of dividend income that recurs every year for as long as that investor continues to retain ownership of those stocks.

This book is designed to teach you exactly how to begin investing within the Nigerian Stock Market. You'll also learn how to identify good value stocks worth holding for the long term that will also yield a healthy level of repeat income.

Brief History of the Nigerian Stock Market

The Nigerian Stock Exchange (NSE) was established back in 1960 and was originally

known as the Lagos Stock Exchange.
For the past 50 years, it has grown to become
Africa's fastest growing Stock Exchange. It
also holds a long history for having been the
most profitable.

The NSE is regulated by the Securities and
Exchange Commission. This offers investors
a certain peace of mind that the market is
monitored and regulated in an effort to avoid
any unfair trading practices and to deter any
manipulations within the market.

The NSE is also a member of the World
Federation of Exchanges (WFE – formerly the
FIBV). This is the international organization
for securities and derivative markets.

The Nigerian Government encourages
investment from international investors. They
actively abolished the legislation that once
prevented international investors from
injecting money into the Nigerian economy.
This abolition means that foreign brokers can
elect to enlist as dealers on the NSE. Foreign
investors of any nationality are now able to
invest in the Nigerian Stock Market easily.

NSE-listed companies are encouraged to create multiple listings for their stocks in other African Stock Exchanges as well as on foreign Stock Exchanges. This increases their trading range and can help to increase their value to investors in some instances.

Trading times and hours for the NSE are a little more limited than larger markets. The NSE operates from 9.30am to 4.30pm Monday to Friday.

Trading fees and charges for trading on the Nigerian Stock Exchange are also considerably lower than many local markets and brokerages. At this time, the charges are as follows:

- 3% commission on the traded value of stocks
- 1% Securities and Exchange Commission fee

Foreign investors may be subjected to a 10% withholding tax on dividend incomes, which is still an extremely competitive rate.

The differences in exchange rate over to Nigerian Naira represent further opportunities to enter the market at relatively low local currency capital amounts. Yet, there is the opportunity to benefit from the fluctuations present between the NGN and most other global currencies.

Trading vs. Investing

Trading is the new buzzword when it comes to the stock market and investing has become a term associated with retirees or people who are not "in" with the times. After all, the whole point of the stock market is to buy low and sell high, right. Why wait for years to see a trickle of a return through dividends when you can make an instant killing by purchasing stocks dirt-cheap and then turning around and selling them the next day for a profit.

Everyone on Wall Street is doing it so they must know something. After all, they are experts, right? What the experts on Wall Street don't tell you is that they will happily trade with their clients' money but prefer investing with their own because of the lower level of risk.

The first thing you need to understand is the difference between trading and investing. Nowadays, most people consider trading to be short-term, i.e. buying stocks and selling them the same day or within a few days, weeks or months at most. In fact, if you've held on to equity for a few months, you are already bordering on being an investor. But we'll consider trading any form of transaction in which the end goal is to make a quick profit from the purchase and sale of a company's shares within a relatively short time frame. On the other hand, when you invest in stock, you are looking at the bigger picture. Your goal is to make as good a return on your investment as possible, which often means considering dividends and not just share price. Sadly, though, even many investors overlook the importance and value of dividends nowadays, focusing solely on share price. But dividends offer the best of both worlds because dividend stocks will offer an immediate return through dividend payouts, as well as a long term one through share price appreciation, with a medium to low level of risk involved.

Choosing a Wealth Creation Strategy

The real key to building true wealth in any market or investment portfolio is to create a strategy before you begin. It's vitally important to assess your own wealth-creation goals and your perceived time span prior to beginning. This will give you a much clearer view of your own investment activities and the level of return you will need to achieve to reach the goals you've set. Wealth creation can take many forms, but the most commonly sought after is capital gain. The vast majority of investors seek to invest their money into an investment vehicle and then see that original amount of capital rise to a larger value.

While there is nothing wrong with this particular strategy, it does leave out one crucial element of wealth creation that really can provide the cornerstone of any investment portfolio: *income*.

Consider this: buying stocks at a low value and then selling them again at a higher value represents profit in the form of capital growth. Once you sink your money into that particular investment, you are required to wait until the values have altered sufficiently before selling that investment again to realize the gains in your account.

This can be a highly successful investment strategy for many people. Yet, the moment you stop trading your stocks, your profits also stop. In this effect, trading becomes a job rather than a true vehicle for wealth creation.

What's more, there's never any guarantee that the value of the stocks you buy will rise in price. They may drop in value instead, leaving you with a loss rather than a profit. This type of trading is highly speculative and can carry plenty of risks.

Investing for Income

However, if you were to invest for the purpose of deriving a solid income that repeats every six months or twelve months, it becomes much easier to see true gains from your initial investment over and over again.

Stockholders have the opportunity to earn dividend yields from the shares in companies they own. As each of the listed companies posts a profit for the financial year, those profits in turn are divided up to pay to the stockholders. As your portfolio of stocks held grows, so too does the amount of income derived from stockholdings.

These same principles work across every stock market in the world. An investor will research which particular stock to purchase and then make a decision whether to sell that stock for the capital profit or whether to hold that stock for the dividend income he can earn.

For as long as you hold a portfolio of performing stocks, you should receive a dividend yield on a regular basis. This can be the ideal way to create an income that continues for however long you own those stocks, yet you also still own the initial investment, so you benefit in two ways.

On top of this, even if the initial value you paid for your stocks goes down, you still continue to receive a dividend return. This means you still reap the profits, regardless of whether your stock values rise or fall. This helps to reduce much of the risk of investing in the stock market.

Investing in Foreign Equities

Researching the New York Stock Exchange for stocks offering a high-yielding dividend payment might feel like a safer option to some people. After all, you're trading stocks owned by local companies that trade locally. Unfortunately, the rate of return is often much lower than you might expect for such large corporations. Despite the stock market prices being low following the crash of 2008/2009, it can still be quite expensive to invest enough money into the market to build up a solid portfolio that will really generate the level of income you hope to receive.

This is where setting your sights a little further afield can help to speed up your wealth creation strategy enormously.

The Nigerian Stock Market suffered a massive crash during January 2009. This meant the value of the vast majority of listed stocks dropped in price, making them much cheaper to buy in. Yet, the dividend yields barely altered.

To a seasoned investor, this type of market situation represents opportunity. Investors have the chance to purchase stocks at cheap prices as compared to their true value, but they also have the advantage of earning very high yields on dividends. This aspect alone makes Nigerian stock market very attractive to investors.

Unfortunately, many newer investors don't have the confidence to invest outside of local borders. This is where it's important to recognize that local brokers can elect to enlist as a broker on foreign stock exchanges, such as the Nigerian Stock Exchange.

Dealing with a broker allows you to ask questions and keep on top of your investments, but still gives you the freedom to invest in the NSE.

You also have the benefit of choosing to use an online broker. This may give you broader access to more individual NSE stocks than just the market indices the majority of brokers may prefer to use.

What's more, the difference in currency value between the Nigerian Naira (NGN) and the US Dollar (USD) also means that it's possible to spend quite a lot of money on the Nigerian Stock Exchange and buy a large number of stocks for a relatively small amount of money in US dollars. This represents the ideal way to begin a true wealth creation strategy for a relatively small amount of money to get started.

Begin with the End in Mind

Once a specific level of wealth has been reached, it's important to have a clear understanding of precisely what you expect to do with that money and how you intend to exit the market.

When you have decided on an investment strategy to help you build wealth, it is always a good idea to consider your exit strategy. Not everyone wants to continue the wealth-building phase of a strategy forever.

In fact, there will come a time when you want to recoup your investment and put it towards other things. This could be put towards funding or supplementing retirement savings, investing in other avenues, or simply using it for other wealth creation purposes.

Regardless of the intent, your exit strategy should form a solid part of your initial investment goals. This may mean selling off your entire investment portfolio and retaining the cash. It may mean selling a portion of your portfolio to invest elsewhere, while allowing the remainder of the portfolio to continue generating income. It's completely up to you what your own strategy should include.

Estate Planning and Tax Obligations

Be aware that your exit strategy may also need to include elements that cover tax obligations and estate planning obligations. Many investors are happy to bequeath their investment portfolios to family or beneficiaries. Yet, this can't be done unless the correct investing entity and estate planning procedures are in place throughout the wealth creation and active investment phase.

Choosing the Right Stocks to Buy

The Nigerian Stock Market operates in much the same way as any other stock market from around the world. Traders buy and sell stocks of listed companies every day.

Each of the stocks you see is a portion of ownership of a much larger corporation. This means you do have the advantage of researching how that company is performing in terms of income, profits and earnings. Rather than buy a stock based on being "cheap", consider researching for value instead. Ideally, you should isolate a company that has a solid record of earnings and profit that represent great value in terms of stock price.

This can be calculated easily by figuring out the Price to Earnings Ratio (P/E Ratio) and then working out the Dividend Yield of a stock you're considering.

The P/E Ratio is one of the most important numbers an analyst will view in order to work out how the market truly values any particular stock.

Essentially, the P/E Ratio tells an investor precisely what the market is willing to pay for that company's earnings. A high P/E Ratio means the market is happy to pay more money in order to access that company's earnings. This can sometimes be seen as a sign of a company that is expected to perform very well, or that may be expected to see an increase in company earnings. Unfortunately, it can also be an indication of an overpriced stock.

On the other hand, a low P/E Ratio may be a sign that the market is not confident in that particular company's stock. However, it could also signify a stock that the market has overlooked.

These are the stocks Warren Buffet would call "value stocks", as their price to earnings ratio is relatively low. This can mean a great return from stocks that are relatively cheap to buy in comparison to the amount of dividends paid per share.

Of course, the dividend yield is the rate at which you'll earn money on your investment. If you were to earn dividends that paid you 3% on your money, you might figure you'd be better off putting your money into a bank account paying high interest on deposits.

Yet, if you could find stocks that pay 10% or 20% dividend yields, this could represent a healthy way to increase your stock portfolio very quickly.

Calculating the P/E Ratio

The P/E Ratio calculation is very simple. You simply take the price of the stock and you divide it by the company's earnings per share.

So if you have a stock trading at $40 and the earnings per share is 8, the calculation is as follows:

$40 / 8 = P/E Ratio 5

Calculating the Dividend Yield

The dividend yield is an important consideration, especially if you intend to use dividends to help you build a solid investment portfolio designed for wealth creation. This is also sometimes called the dividend-price ratio.

The yield is the rate at which you will be rewarded for holding a particular stock. Essentially, it is the company's total dividend payments each year divided by the dividend paid per share, divided by the price per share. The resulting figure is displayed as a percentage.

So, if a stock is trading at $40 and the dividend paid is $2 per share, the yield would be calculated as follows:

Full-Year Dividend / Current Share Price = Dividend Yield

$2 / $40 = 0.05 = 5%

Essentially, this means you'll receive a 5% return on your investment. If this is higher than you could receive by sticking your money in a bank account and earning 1% interest, it can't be all bad.

5% isn't an extraordinarily high return for a stock dividend yield, especially when there are banks in Australia and New Zealand paying investors more than 6% just for depositing cash in a bank account in January 2012.

There is no right or wrong yield percentage, only the rate at which you're comfortable investing your money and at which you want to see it grow. For wealth creation purposes, the yield you choose should represent a rate of return that allows you to earn a decent dividend amount from your initial investment that will also increase your portfolio holdings. This is the true key to effective wealth creation.

Calculating the Price-to-sales Ratio

The price-to-sales ratio or PSR is similar to the P/E except that you are working out exactly how much you are paying per dollar of sales instead of profits.

So, you first need to calculate total sales per share, which is done by dividing the total outstanding shares into the total volume of sales.

Sales per share = Total Sales / Outstanding Shares

Thus, if a company has made $40 million in sales and has 4 million outstanding shares, then the sales per share are $10. To calculate the price to sales ratio, you will divide the share price by the sales per share. So, if the shares of the company in our example were selling for $25, then the PSR would be 2.5.

Generally, shares with a PSR of two or less are considered undervalued. As a rule of thumb, you want to find stocks that are undervalued both in PSR and P/E to ensure you are getting good bargain.

Building Wealth with Small Amounts to Get Started

One of the primary reasons to invest in the Nigerian Stock Market is the high rate of return on dividend yields compared to the relatively low price of their stocks.

Of course, another valid reason is the benefit most people in the developed countries have to enter the stock market with such a small amount of capital to get started. They simply would not have the same level of opportunity to build wealth in local markets using such low amounts of money.

When you add these two factors together, you have a situation where it should cost you only a small sum of money to get started, but your returns are high enough to see your initial investment grow quickly. This still remains true no matter whether the market is rising or falling.

For the purpose of this example, we'll begin with just $1,000 US dollars. That's such a small amount of money to begin building a wealth creation portfolio with, but it

really can grow into a substantial amount of money very quickly if you're careful with your investment strategy.

Another point to note is that beginning your foreign investment strategy with only a small amount of money is a great way to test the market for yourself before investing much larger sums later.

Research Example

To give you a clearer idea of how this can work, let's look at a real stock on the Nigerian Stock Exchange right now.

Remember, this is just an example. It's not a 'hot tip' or a recommendation. We're simply using this company to give you an idea how easy it is to find good value stocks based on research and simple calculations. For the purpose of this example, we'll be using Fidelity Bank (stock ticker: FidelityBK).

At the time of this writing, the Fidelity Bank is trading at around N1.40 per share. It pays a dividend of N0.14 per share.

Calculation	Result
P/E Ratio	6.7

With Dividend Stocks In the Nigerian Stock Market

Dividend Yield   10%

These figures and calculations mean it's a reasonably cheap stock offering a good rate of return on your investment.

A little further research uncovers that the Fidelity Bank has good earnings and only low levels of financial commitments showing on its balance reports.

You can verify this information here: http://www.nigerianstockexchange.com/quoted_company.jsp?symbol=FIDELITYBK

Starting with $1,000 USD

Now we have our example stock lined up and we know we're likely to only pay N1.40 per share.

What does this mean to an American investor, who doesn't have a handy supply of Nigerian Naira sitting in a bank account?

It means we need to work out how many shares you're able to buy in Nigerian Naira (NGN) if you are beginning with only $1,000 USD.

Before you send out your cheque to cover the cost of your trade, you need to work out exactly how much your $1,000 USD will convert to in NGN.

According to www.xe.com $1,000 USD = N 161,800

This means you will be buying approximately 100,000 shares of Fidelity Bank stock.

Transaction	Cost
Stock Price per share	**N1.40**
100,000 shares	**N140,000**
3% commission	**N4200**

With Dividend Stocks In the Nigerian Stock Market

1% Securities and Exchange Commission Fee	**N1400**
Total Cost for this trade	**N145,600**

This amount (N145,600) is under $900 USD, yet you will own 100,000 shares of a large Nigerian Bank. That's the start of a healthy portfolio.

For those investors who are nervous investing in a foreign stock exchange, this offers a great way to enter the market without risking large amounts of capital. Over time as you monitor your initial investment, you should notice that nothing terrible is happening to your money. Once you build that level of confidence and trust with your money being invested in Nigeria, you then have the opportunity to buy more stocks, add to your portfolio,

and increase your exposure to the market as far as you wish.

With Dividend Stocks In the Nigerian Stock Market

Remember: foreign currency exchange fees may apply. Always check what rate you will be charged in fees for exchanging your local currency over to Nigerian Naira.

Taking Advantage of the Reduced Stock Prices

It's no secret that the Nigerian Stock Exchange has taken a bit of a beating in recent times. In fact, even a small amount of research on a basic Google search will show you that activity within the Nigerian Stock Market has slowed right down.

As a result, prices of some previously valuable stocks showing high dividend yields have dropped to extremely low rates.

To some investors, this can be cause for alarm. They worry that the market is failing or that the stocks aren't worth much, and so they tend to shy away from investing at all.

However, a savvy investor knows that a falling market is a sign of good opportunity.

Think about it: if prices for stocks of profitable companies are selling very cheaply, this represents a good opportunity to enter the market at a lower cost to you.

Likewise, if the prices are low, but the value and earnings of the underlying company is much higher than indicated, this represents the ideal situation in which prices are likely to rise.

Buying into the stock market while stock prices are at rock bottom can be an excellent way to begin building up your share portfolio. You'll have large volumes of shares on your account that you paid a relatively cheap price for.

However, once the market does start to recover and the prices rise, the value of your existing share holdings will increase dramatically. Many highly profitable investors base their entire investment strategies based on this one single factor.

Check Historical Data

Before buying any stock on any stock market, it's always wise to spend a little time analyzing the historical data for that stock. You should be able to find charts and trading prices for any stock you're considering very easily.

The object of this exercise isn't to 'buy cheap and sell high'. Rather, you want to buy value and hold for dividend income. In order to do this, you first need to identify what represents value for your own investing purposes.

If you have stock trading software, use this to try and identify any trend lines in the pricing history. You should notice that almost every single stock listed on the Nigerian Stock

Exchange fell in value during 2009. Some of those have made a little recovery. Others are still working their way back up the pricing scale.

Regardless, it's important to note that the rate of return, or dividend yield, is noticeably higher when the stock you want to purchase is being sold so cheaply. This helps you build up your portfolio and increase your passive income much faster, as you're paying less money to get started, but you're reaping a high return at the same time.

Slower Activity – Lower Liquidity?

One of the problems with a stock market facing slower trading activity is the risk of lower liquidity. If you purchase a stock with the intention of selling it for a profit, low liquidity will become a huge problem, especially if there aren't enough buyers out there waiting to buy what you're selling.

If you're keen to sell off your investment after only a relatively short time in the market, you may need to be patient until enough buyers show up to buy the stocks you want to sell.

Don't be fooled into thinking that a 'slow liquidity' period means no one is buying at all. This isn't true. It's just a lot slower currently than it once was, but it is showing signs of recovery, with more active investors returning to the market.

While liquidity might be reduced in the current Nigerian Stock market, this shouldn't affect a smart investor. After all, the key to building a strong portfolio is to hold stocks over the long term to reap the dividend yields. Liquidity becomes less of an issue when you're working with this particular strategy.

The Nigerian Stock Market: Perfect for Value Investors

The Nigerian stock market can be an excellent source of these hidden gems for value investors because it is an emerging market and it is not considered a trendy investment at the moment. This means that you will find plenty of under appreciated stocks with an excellent dividend yield and payout that can make for some amazing returns in the long run.

For example, the chart below, which had the dividend yield of approximately 6.9% for 2011. As you can see, even though the price of the stock has depreciated since the boom before 2008, over a five-year period it has still seen growth from its initial trading price before the spike.

Please note that this is not a recommendation, just an example of how you can benefit from investing in the Nigerian stock market.

With Dividend Stocks In the Nigerian Stock Market

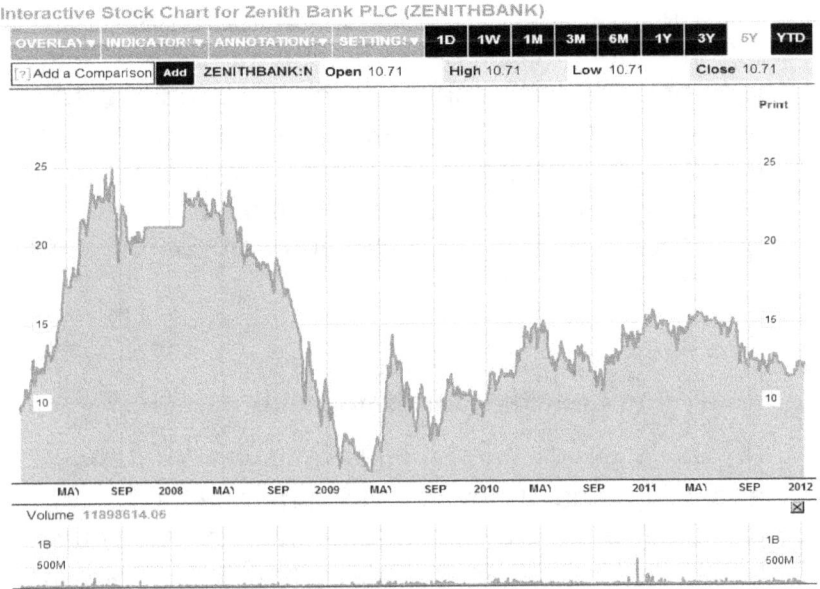

Chart Courtesy of Bloomberg.com

The Company: Facts and Figures

A company that is publicly traded is legally required to publish key facts and figures that reveal the company's performance or lack thereof. A company's annual report will usually contain all the year-end financial statements you need to make an effective evaluation.

Quarterly reports are also a good source of information and can help you stay up-to-date with a company's performance without having to wait for the end of the fiscal year to see the company's results. These reports are usually available on company websites. If the information is unavailable on their website, you can contact them and request a copy.

Analyzing Company Fundamentals

So, what should you be looking at when you are analyzing a company? Buying shares in a company means that you actually own part of that company, no matter how many or few shares you purchase. Think of it like lending a friend money to start a new business. If your friend were virtually bankrupt because he or she can't manage their personal finances properly, then you would probably be reluctant to lend them the money. The same goes for a company.

To determine how financially sound a company is and to ensure the management knows what they are doing, you need to analyze three documents, namely the balance sheet, income statement and cash flow statement. The numbers found in these documents constitute the fundamentals of the company. Once you understand this fundamental information, you can compare the results and calculate specific ratios to help you determine how healthy a company is and make a reasonably accurate forecast of how the company will continue to perform.

Understanding the Balance Sheet

The balance sheet shows exactly what a company owns (assets) and what debts it has (liabilities), usually at the end of each quarter. It's referred to as a balance sheet because total assets must equal liabilities with total shareholder equity. That's a fancy way of saying that whatever the company owns and isn't being used to pay debts is owned by the stockholders. Below is an example of a balance sheet. It is the actual balance sheet for 2009 and 2010 for Zenith Bank Nigeria. As you can see, the company has a wide range of assets, which include

cash, accounts receivables, treasury bonds, properties, equipment and so on.

BALANCE SHEETS

AS AT 31 DECEMBER 2010	Group 2010 N'million	Group 2009 N'million	Bank 2010 N'million	Bank 2009 N'million
ASSETS				
Cash and balances with central banks	141,724	126,779	130,604	115,044
Treasury bills	298,869	234,115	287,981	225,371
Due from other banks	399,503	341,830	374,604	290,025
Loans and advances	713,285	698,326	667,860	669,261
On-lending facilities	22,536	-	22,536	-
Advances under finance lease	13,188	5,506	12,731	5,281
Insurance receivables	711	635	-	-
Investment securities	210,345	158,977	171,985	144,189
Investment in subsidiaries	-	-	37,134	36,096
Deferred tax assets	1,162	966	-	-
Other assets	18,936	13,517	13,470	12,758
Investment property	7,623	433	7,036	-
Property and equipment	67,145	78,619	63,517	75,171
Total assets	1,895,027	1,659,703	1,789,458	1,573,196
Liabilities				
Customers' deposits	1,318,072	1,173,917	1,289,552	1,111,328
Claims payable	218	198	-	-
Liabilities on insurance contracts	2,287	1,202	-	-
On-lending facilities	26,049	-	26,049	-
Borrowings	27,975	35,984	27,975	35,984
Current income tax	3,735	7,407	1,010	5,718
Other liabilities	145,750	100,085	87,314	88,683
Deferred income tax liabilities	7,380	3,117	7,144	3,100
Total liabilities	1,531,466	1,321,910	1,439,044	1,244,813
Capital and reserves				
Share capital	15,698	12,559	15,698	12,559
Share premium	255,047	255,047	255,047	255,047
Revaluation reserve	98	-	-	-
Retained earnings	62,610	44,883	51,307	37,415
Other reserves	27,789	23,081	28,362	23,362
Attributable to equity holders of the parent	361,242	335,570	350,414	328,383
Non-controlling interest	2,319	2,223	-	-
Total shareholders' equity	363,561	337,793	350,414	328,383
Total Liabilities and equity	1,895,027	1,659,703	1,789,458	1,573,196
Acceptances and guarantees	902,931	638,708	866,169	606,594

Assets

Essentially, anything that has value and is owned by the company is considered to be an asset. In turn, assets can be categorized into four types, namely current assets, investments, fixed assets and intangibles.

Current assets refer to any type of asset that can quickly be converted into cash. These include cash, of course, and all forms of cash equivalents such as bank accounts, money market accounts, treasury bills and so on. Accounts receivables, namely funds the company is owed through unsettled bills on goods or services that have already been provided, as well as the value of everything a company has ready to sell are also considered current assets.

Investments are another form of assets but these are specifically long-term investments such as stocks, bonds or derivatives. They cannot easily be converted to cash or they would fall under the current asset section. Fixed assets include buildings, vehicles and equipment. Essentially, anything that physically exists and has a long life, which the company needs to operate, is considered a fixed asset.

Intangible assets refer to anything that has value but is not involved in the production of the goods or services the company sells. These include patents, trademarks, licenses and so on.

Liabilities

Liabilities refer to any debts the company has to other entities. While most people consider debt a bad thing, in this case it isn't always true because you really do need to spend money to make money. The problem arises when a company is always spending more than it is making.

So, in terms of liabilities, these are split up into current, long-term and other liabilities. Current liabilities represent all short-term debt that must be cleared with the year. Long-term liabilities refer to any loans the company has to pay back over a period that is longer than twelve months. Lastly, other liabilities are any other debts the company has.

Shareholder Equity

Shareholder equity is also known as the company's net worth and is exactly what the stockholders own after all debts have been paid off. It's calculated as the difference between assets and liabilities.

It is important to understand the balance sheet because we will be using these numbers later on to determine the financial health of a company.

The Income Statement or Profit and Loss Statement

The income statement is a report that shows all the company's expenses and revenues. Namely, how much the company is making from sales and how much the company is spending.

The final figure is the net income of the company in question and if it is positive, it means the company is making a profit, if it's negative, the company is losing money and zero means it's breaking even. While this is quite clear, there is also some other vital information available in a P&L statement.

Some of the more important figures include:

Gross revenues

Cost of goods sold, which represents how much it costs to purchase raw materials and produce the final product;

Gross profit, which is calculated as the difference between total revenues and total cost of goods sold;

Gross Profit Margin is calculated by dividing the gross profit by total revenues. This is an important number that you will use often when deciding whether or not to invest in a certain dividend stock. Generally, you want to look for companies with a gross profit margin over 50%;

Overheads, which include selling costs, administrative costs and general costs.

These are all the expenses required to keep the business running;

Operating income is calculated as the difference between gross profit and overheads;

Earnings before interest, taxes, depreciation and amortization (EBITDA) is usually a combination of operating income with any income from long-term investments;

Interest expenses;

Non-operating income, which represents any earnings that didn't result from business operations, such as investments or the sale of an asset;

Earnings from continuing operations;

Earnings from discontinued operations;

Net Income, which represents the real profit after all possible expenses have been deducted. This number is also commonly referred to as the bottom line because it really is the last line in a P&L statement.

Below is the Profit and Loss Statement of Zenith Bank for 2009 and 2010.

PROFIT AND LOSS ACCOUNTS

FOR THE YEAR ENDED 31 DECEMBER 2010	12 Months Group 2010 N'million	15 Months Group 2009 N'million	12 Months Bank 2010 N'million	15 Months Bank 2009 N'million
Gross earnings	192,486	277,300	169,370	254,147
Interest and similar income	127,265	193,545	118,491	186,019
Interest and similar expenses	(35,719)	(83,957)	(34,522)	(82,836)
Net interest income	91,546	109,588	83,969	103,183
Fee and commission income	46,180	55,014	39,885	49,830
Underwriting income	7,145	7,450	-	-
Underwriting expenses	(4,621)	(5,105)	-	-
Underwriting profit	2,524	2,345	-	-
Foreign exchange trading income	10,823	19,687	9,743	17,369
Trusteeship income	45	42	-	-
Income from investments	304	1,326	455	484
Other income	726	236	795	445
Operating income	152,148	188,238	134,848	171,311
Operating expenses	(97,769)	(113,288)	(89,074)	(103,410)
Diminution in asset values	(4,353)	(39,865)	(2,817)	(36,148)
Profit before tax	50,026	35,085	42,957	31,753
Taxation	(12,612)	(14,482)	(9,622)	(13,388)
Profit after tax	37,414	20,603	33,335	18,365
Non controlling interest	(84)	(106)	-	-
Profit attributable to Group shareholders	37,330	20,497	33,335	18,365
Key Financial Information				
Total non-performing loans and advances (N'million)	44,271	48,379	41,832	46,413
Total non-performing loans to total loans and advances (%)	5.93%	6.47%	6.00%	6.48%
Earnings per share (basic)	119 k	82 k	106 k	73 k
Earnings per share (adjusted)	119 k	65 k	106 k	58 k
Dividend per share (proposed)	85 k	45 k	85 k	45 k

Cash Flow Statement

The cash flow statement shows the movement of all cash in a company. Essentially, it shows where the money is coming from and whether or not it has been paid. It also shows where the money is going and whether or not the company physically spent more money than it made.

Cash flow can make or break a company, even if it is profitable. A negative cash flow means the company is paying out more than it is taking in and this isn't always the result of poor sales but of failure to collect accounts receivable. The problem is that a company can grind to a halt if it can't cover the cost of goods sold because then it won't have the raw materials to produce the goods and will end up with nothing to sell. This is how many companies have gone bankrupt.

It is essential for a company to have some free cash flow to cover unexpected costs. In fact, the free cash flow should exceed the amount of money the company pays out in dividends and interest. The more free cash flow a company has, the more secure the dividend payout will be. If a company borrows funds to pay dividends, it will end up digging itself into a hole it will have serious trouble climbing out of so make sure the company has plenty of free cash before purchasing dividend stocks.

Adding to Your Portfolio

Beginning your wealth creation portfolio with a small amount of money is a great way to get started. It helps you get a feel for the market and its particular movements. It helps you reduce the worry and uncertainty of having money invested in a foreign country.

It also helps you to realize that many foreign countries represent excellent investment opportunities for those who go looking for them.

Once you have noticed that investing money into the heavily regulated Nigerian Stock Exchange actually does return a profit, you may decide to invest a little more of your money.

If you've chosen a broker to place your trades, you can then instruct them on the stock you want to be added to your portfolio.

Investing on a Budget

For those people trying to build up a wealth-creation portfolio on a budget, the Nigerian Stock Exchange represents an ideal solution. As mentioned earlier in this chapter, you have the unique opportunity to purchase large volumes of stocks at very low capital costs.

As you can afford it, you have the freedom to purchase more stocks across other sectors when it suits you. You might decide to purchase $500 USD worth of banking stocks one month and another $500 USD worth of healthcare stocks another.

While this may not seem like a huge amount of money in developed countries, these are quite hefty sums of money in Nigeria that will buy plenty of stocks of some very large and profitable companies. Even those people on low incomes can suddenly afford to create wealth-building stock portfolios using the NSE.

Of course, if you have more money to invest, be sure to calculate your own investment goals and invest the amount you are comfortable with.

The higher dividend yields available on the Nigerian Stock Exchange do represent an opportunity to build retirement savings quickly, but there's also the advantage of turning that portfolio into an income-producing store of wealth.

With Dividend Stocks In the Nigerian Stock Market

Understanding Dividends

Dividends are payments companies make to their shareholders, essentially dividing up a share of the profits the company has made. When you purchase a share in a company, you are basically lending the company money and, in return, the company pledges to pay you a share of the profits they make, in the form of dividends.

However, not all companies pay out dividends, especially if they are not performing well, but there are other factors that influence this. For example, some companies feel it is better to reinvest as large a portion of the profits as possible to drive company growth, which in turn benefits shareholders by driving up the value of the company and, implicitly the value of its stock. Thus, shareholders benefit when they sell their shares by making a hefty profit – the buy low, sell high principles.

Then there are companies who believe that shareholders actually own the company and should benefit directly from the profits the company makes. And these are the companies we will be focusing on because dividend investing has plenty of advantages, especially for the retail investor.

The Benefits and Risks of Dividends

So, what exactly are the benefits of dividends? Investing in dividend stocks is like putting money in the bank and receiving interest on it. The difference is that dividends usually offer a better rate of return than simply open a savings account and waiting for the bank to decide on the level of interest you will receive.

While investing in dividends is not quite as exciting as watching the price of stocks rise and fall and it certainly can't provide the same level of profits, it also doesn't pose such a high level of risk. Investing in dividend stocks offers investors two ways to profit, namely from share price appreciation as well as dividend payouts. These types of shares usually experience a lower degree of volatility in share price, even when the market falls but also when the market is booming. However, there is a much lower risk of you losing your entire investment in one afternoon, even if the profits are slower to come in.

Investing in dividend stock means you are setting up a stream of steady passive income, which you can then spend or reinvest, depending on your overall strategy. It's an ideal way to create a nest egg for retirement, which you can control directly. It is also an ideal vehicle to create wealth, especially if you start early and reinvest all the dividends you earn in shares. As with any investment strategy, remember that you want to have a diverse portfolio but we'll get into that a little more later on.

Companies that pay out dividends are usually more stable than those that don't. A company that is just starting up is unlikely to pay dividends because their full focus is on reinvesting to fuel growth.

Dividends only come onto the scene once the company has matured and reached a sustainable level of profitability. A dividend-paying company's management is also less likely to take unwarranted risks because they are more accountable to shareholders. If they've promised to pay out dividends and none are forthcoming, they will have to explain themselves.

Another advantage to investing in dividend stocks is that you are collecting profit without selling the shares. This also makes it much easier to grow your investment because with non-dividend paying stocks, even if share prices go up, your profits are still locked up in the shares. With dividend stocks, you can use the dividends to purchase more shares, which automatically increases the profit you make and you can compound this until you end up with a nice nest egg for the future. You will own assets that have their own value but still produce a profit in cash on a regular basis.

Dividends can often be used as a hedge against inflation. The payout is determined as a ratio of profit levels and most companies increase prices to adjust for inflation rates. This means that inflation won't cut into your profits as it would if you simply relied on a savings account or by investing in non-dividend paying stocks. While the increased dividend payout might not always fully offset the inflation rate, it still goes a long way towards reducing its impact on your earnings.

Another very important benefit is that more often than not dividend stocks continue paying out dividends even in a bear market. So, you can still make a profit, even if the value of the shares themselves is dropping.

Of course, nothing is perfect and dividend stocks still come with their own share of risks. You can still lose money by investing in dividend stocks because there is no investment that is 100% safe. For example, the price of shares can drop significantly, even if it does pay out dividends, and the worst-case scenario is for the company to declare bankruptcy before you have a chance to offload your shares.

Another risk you will be exposing yourself to is that companies have no legal obligation to pay dividends, which means they can reduce payments or stop them altogether. Note, though, that most companies try to avoid slashing dividends unless they have no other option because shareholders will often sell their shares as quickly as possible, which will drive down the price.

You also have to take inflation into consideration when investing in dividend stocks. Your investment has to keep pace with the rate of inflation or every penny you invest will be worth much less. This is why you also need to take inflation rate into consideration when calculating the rate or return on your investment. For example, if the ROI seems to be 7 percent, remember to deduct the inflation rate to work out how much money you are really making. If the inflation rate is 2.5 percent, then your actual profit is 4.5 percent.

While there is a chance you could lose your investment, the reality is that dividend investing is one of the safest forms of investments and an excellent vehicle to grow your wealth.

With Dividend Stocks In the Nigerian Stock Market

Dividend Investing For Income: What to Look For

When you invest in dividend stocks, your goal is to create a passive income while at the very least preserving your capital. In the best-case scenario, though, you want to see a little capital appreciation as well. So, what should you be looking for when deciding on which dividend stocks are the best for establishing healthy passive income?

First of all, you want to analyze the dividend yield. This is the return on your investment, as a percentage, that comes solely from dividends. For example, if you buy shares for $50 apiece and the company is paying out dividends of $2.5 per share every year that means your annual return on investment is 5%. However, remember to take into account the inflation rate, which will reduce your profitability.

So, presuming the inflation rate is 2.5%, and then your actual ROI is 2.5% per annum per share. This means that you want to target shares that have a dividend yield higher than 4% so you are actually seeing a profit.

Another figure you want to look at is the percentage of profits the company allocates toward dividend payments, also known as the payout ratio. Generally, anything higher than 50% is a good bet but if the company is paying out over 100%, you should start worrying because the money is coming from somewhere and that's not from profit.

You also want to look at dividend growth, which is often more important than the yield, if a company has steadily been increasing its dividend payouts, it means that its profitability has been increasing every year. This shows sustainability for the long-term and it's exactly what you want to invest in.

Often, you can make a higher profit from a company paying a low dividend yield and consistent growth than you can from one with a higher yield but no growth. Remember, you are looking at the bigger picture here and not what you can make in the first year or even two.

With Dividend Stocks In the Nigerian Stock Market

Using Dividends to Build Wealth Faster

In the example from an earlier research, we established that the dividend yield on our example stock, Fidelity Bank, was 10%. We also bought 100,000 shares for under $900 USD at a cost of N1.40 per share.

When you purchase any stocks across any stock market, you should be given an option to receive the dividends as a payment directly to you or your account. You should also be given an option for 'dividend reinvestment'. In some markets, this may also be known as 'dividend reallocation'.

This simply means you choose not to receive those dividends as income – yet.

Rather, you choose to let the company reinvest the amount of money you would have earned in the form of additional stocks. The company calculates how many stocks you could buy with the amount of dividend payment you could have received and that number of stocks is added to your portfolio automatically.

Effectively, this builds your portfolio for you on autopilot every time a dividend payment is issued. It means you don't need to keep putting your own money into your portfolio in order to see it grow. It also means you don't need to pay brokerage fees or commissions to purchase more stock, as those additional stocks are allocated to you automatically.

Description	Value
Initial number of stocks	100,000
Value of initial stocks	N140,000
Dividend Yield	10%
Number of stocks added to portfolio	14,000
Total number of stocks owned after dividend payment	110,000

Total value of portfolio after dividend payment (@N1.40 per share)	**N154,000**

This growth in your portfolio cost you no extra money out of your pocket, yet it did increase your wealth automatically for you. This strategy works very well for any investor willing to remain in the market long enough to allow the dividends to automatically grow a portfolio over time.

Your portfolio for this stock only after 3 years of doing nothing but owning them would look like this:

Transaction	Cost
Initial number of shares	**100,000**
+ 10% dividend reallocation 10,000	**110,000**

stocks	
+10% dividend reallocation 11,000 stocks	**121,000**
+10% dividend reallocation 12,100 stocks	**133,100**
Total Number of stocks owned	**133,100**
Total portfolio value (@N1.40 per share)	**N186,340**

This example assumes that the dividend yield doesn't alter throughout that 3-year period. Yet, the reality is that most dividend yields do change. Many increase as company profits increase.

This example also didn't take into account any pricing increases in the value of that stock over three years. Even based on completely static numbers, it's still evident that your investment portfolio increased automatically, simply because you reinvested the dividend earnings back into the market.

Imagine what your portfolio would be worth if the stock value also rose in value throughout that same time? It becomes much easier to see how you can easily double or even triple your portfolio value in a relatively short period of time.

While the numbers in this example might look low, imagine how they'd look if you'd begun your investing with a larger amount of money? Imagine getting started with $10,000 or $100,000. The results would be a little more impressive then.

Of course, the results would be even more impressive if we'd chosen a stock returning a 20% dividend yield. For the purpose of the example, we chose an average yielding stock, but the Nigerian Stock Exchange is renowned for offering some incredibly high yielding stocks. It all comes down to your research. The amount of profit you make is all relative to the initial amount you invest, so keep in mind it's not about the dollars, but about how you choose to keep your money growing.

This is why calculating the rate of return is so vitally important to your wealth creation goals. Choosing stocks carefully that are likely to return very good dividend yields just increases your investment portfolio faster with every dividend payment you choose to reinvest.

Any good investor knows that it can take time to build a portfolio of this level, so be patient and stick to your long-term goals. The results will be worth the effort.

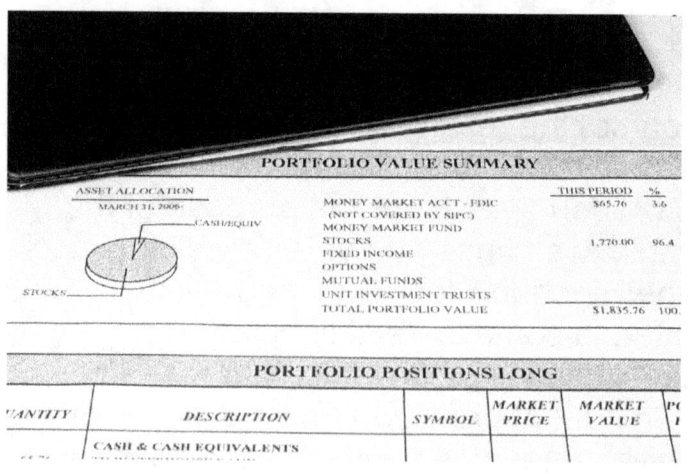

Investing for Income

In order to really begin generating an income from dividends, you will need to have a portfolio containing sufficient stocks that pay a generous dividend yield. There are two ways to build your portfolio to this level:

1) Invest more of your own cash

2) Learn to build your portfolio using dividends until it is large enough to generate income.

Allowing your dividend earnings to be reinvested back into your portfolio is the wealth creation side of your investing strategy. Once your portfolio has reached a size where the dividends you earn represent a healthy supplemental income, you don't need to keep reinvesting them. You can simply choose to have those earnings sent to you directly instead, either via cheque or into your account.

We looked at how you can use your dividend earnings to build your wealth creation portfolio relatively quickly in the previous chapter. However, there's nothing stopping you from adding to your stock portfolio when you have the extra funds to invest. This will simply speed up your wealth creation plans.

Who Gets the Dividends?

When you buy stocks from any stock market in the world, there are two terms you need to watch for. These are:

- ✓ Ex Dividend (XD); and
- ✓ Cum Dividend (CD)

Ex Dividend (XD)

Most stocks will be classified as "Ex Dividend" shortly before the actual dividend payment is due to be made by the company. This allows the company to calculate accurately who is receiving a cheque and who will be receiving a dividend reallocation/reinvestment. It also means that if you purchase a stock while it is Ex Dividend, you won't receive the dividends due on that particular stock during this payment cycle. The previous owner will. You will need to wait until the next time dividends are issued to receive your share.

Conversely, if you sell your stocks during the Ex Dividend, you still receive your dividend earnings, but the buyer of those stocks won't.

Once the dividend payments and allocations have been made, the stock should immediately turn Cum Dividend again.

Cum Dividend (CD)

Cum Dividend simply means "with dividend". When you buy or sell any stock, it trades as Cum Dividend right up until the Ex Dividend Date.

Obviously, if you're investing in order to grow your portfolio using your dividends or to receive income from your dividend earnings, it makes sense to check that any stocks you buy are trading as Cum Dividend wherever possible.

You should also keep in mind that not all stocks pay dividends. Always check and re-check that the stock you intend to purchase does pay dividends. Check the dividend payment date and the Ex Dividend date before purchasing.

Dividend Payment Date

The fun part about earning an income from dividends is that not every company pays out their dividend earnings on the same date.

If you own a range of stocks across multiple sectors and industries, it's very possible to put together a very strong investment portfolio where you receive a cheque in the mail every month.

Many companies pay out their dividends once or twice a year. By choosing the right stocks, it's possible to spread your dividend earnings throughout the year.

Diversifying Your Portfolio

A wise investor knows that a well-diversified portfolio can act as a hedge against any sudden drops in stock value occurring in any sector of the stock market.

For example, when the market reacts to news, the stock values for entire industry sectors can be affected equally. So, if one bank in Nigeria reports problems, the stocks for most banks in the sector may suffer from reduced stock values.

For this reason, it can be wise to research stocks across several different sectors. This allows you to retain much – if not all – of the initial value of your investment in the case of one sector falling in value when the others remain strong.

Keeping a strong mix of stocks from various sectors can be an excellent way to reduce volatility. Obviously you want to protect the value of your initial investment as much as possible, but you also want to ensure that you're deriving the best possible yield from the stocks you do hold.

There's also the factor of mixing growth stocks and security stocks in your portfolio to help broaden your exposure and minimize your risk.

Minimize Risk

What's more, diversification is also the ideal tool for helping to minimize your risk.

Consider this: if you held $10,000 USD in just one stock on the Nigerian Stock Exchange and the value of that stock fell dramatically, you risk losing a large portion of your initial investment.

Yet, if you had that same $10,000 spread across four or five industry sectors and the same stock fell dramatically in value, only a portion of your entire portfolio is affected. This helps to keep your potential losses to an absolute minimum, while ensuring that you preserve as much as possible of your initial capital investment amount.

Example 1:

Let's assume you own $10,000 worth of MadeUp Stock. Yes, I just made this up, so let's give it the stock ticker code of MUS.

You bought it at $14.50 per share, which means you own about 689 shares of this stock.

If the value of MUS drops down to $9.50 per share, your portfolio is suddenly only worth $6,545.50. That's a big drop in capital value to your overall investment portfolio.

Example 2:

Let say this time that you only have $2,000 invested in MadeUp Stock, with another $2,000 invested in Strong Stock. You have $2,000 worth of Safe Shares and another $2,000 with GoodDividend Company. The final $2,000 is invested with BigBank Stock.

This still equates to a total portfolio of $10,000, but you've broken it down into five segments across different industry sectors.

In this example, the value of your MadeUp Stock goes down from $14.50 to $9.50, but the rest of your stocks aren't affected. Instead of losing $3,500 off the value of your entire portfolio, you're only risking a drop of $700. That's quite a safety net.

Growth Stocks

Growth stocks are those that show high earnings and high dividend yields. These types of stocks are very tempting for investors, as they feel they're getting better returns on their money.

Growth stocks are an important inclusion for any investor working to build up a portfolio for wealth creation purposes.

Unfortunately, high yields can also sometimes represent higher-than-average risk. You may also find that the prices for these stocks can be somewhat more volatile than lower-risk stocks.

Security Stocks

Opting to keep a portion of your portfolio safe in security stocks is a wise move. You will find that the dividend yield is lower for stocks in this category, but the price of those stocks is also far less volatile as well.

Lower yields do not equate to bad investments. They simply mean you're earning a slightly lower rate of return on your initial investment. If you spent time researching your prices initially, you should find plenty of stocks on the Nigerian Stock Exchange selling far below their true value, but that also make excellent security stocks to add to your overall portfolio.

Building a Well-Diversified Portfolio

The natural instinct of most investors is to look for the highest possible yield they can find and then sink money into these. While having high yielding stocks is always a good idea, it's also important to consider your level of diversification.

Many investment advisors will try to recommend that you choose between 10 and 12 different stocks to hold in your portfolio. For a very large portfolio, this can be wise.

However, for a growth portfolio designed to generate dividend income, choosing 5 or 6 different stocks will be sufficient. Always look for stocks in sectors that people rely on, regardless of what the economy is doing.

For example, you could choose conglomerates companies to form one sector of your diversification plan. Foods, beverages and tobacco companies are another area that can be buffered a little from economic crisis, as people will still need to buy food and other consumer goods.

The rest of your portfolio selections are up to your own discretion and should be strongly based on your research into individual companies.

Using the Foreign Currency Exchange to Build Wealth

The title is a little bit deceptive, as you won't technically be trading foreign currency to build wealth or grow your investment portfolio. You will still be buying and selling stocks on the Nigerian Stock Exchange for the purpose of building a strong portfolio of stocks paying you high-yielding dividend amounts.

However, because the NSE is in a foreign country, there is the natural side effect of benefiting from the fluctuations in the currency exchange rates at any time.

Let's go right back to the first example, where we bought 100,000 shares of Fidelity Bank for under $900 USD:

Transaction	Cost
Stock Price per share	N1.4
100,000 shares	N140,000
3% commission	N4200
1% Securities and Exchange Commission Fee	N1400
Total Cost for this trade	N145,600

Let's assume we held onto these particular stocks for 3 years while we built up your portfolio of other stocks around them.

With Dividend Stocks In the Nigerian Stock Market

Your portfolio for this stock only after 3 years of doing nothing but owning them would look like this:

Transaction	Number of Shares in Portfolio
Initial number of shares	100,000
+ 10% dividend reallocation 10,000 stocks	110,000
+10% dividend reallocation 11,000 stocks	120,100
+10% dividend reallocation 12,100 stocks	133,100
Total Number of stocks owned	133,100

In the original example, we paid N1.40 per share for this particular stock. At the time, the US dollar to Nigerian Naira exchange rate was 1:161.8

Yet, we've allowed three years to pass to show the effects of allowing dividends to reinvest into a portfolio. During those three years, the value of this particular

stock has risen to N2.10 per stock. A strengthening US economy has also seen the Nigerian Naira drop in value against the USD to 1:151.5

Let's see what these changes have done to your portfolio overall.

Your portfolio for this stock only after 3 years of doing nothing but owning them would look like this:

Transaction	Amount
Total Number of stocks owned	**133,100**

Value @ N2.10 per share	**N 279,510**
US Dollar Value of portfolio	**$1,844.95**

Considering you only put $899.80 into purchasing your initial stocks in the first example, to see that your investment has now more than doubled in just 3 years, with you doing nothing at all is brilliant news.

Yes, the increase in stock value does account for some of this profit, but the alteration in the exchange rate between the US dollar and the Nigerian Naira accounts for the rest.

Margin Lending and Wealth Building

Another way you can maximize your earnings and grow your wealth is through margin lending. Before we go any further, though, it is imperative that you understand the inherent risks that come with margin lending.

Essentially, you are borrowing money to buy dividend stocks. Much like a bank will issue a mortgage if you put your house up as security, banks will also issue a margin loan using your owned stocks as security.

Keep in mind that borrowing money to invest is extremely risky and should be approached carefully. Always keep your loan-to-value ratio cautiously low and only ever borrow what you can realistically afford to repay. If you don't take into account market volatility, you could hit a margin call and lose everything. Therefore, you need to take extensive precautions and avoid using this approach with highly volatile stocks.

How Margin Lending Works

The idea behind using margin lending to purchase dividend stocks is to maximize the annual return on your investment, which can be reinvested to further increase your earnings. However, for this approach to be effective, you need to ensure that the interest you are paying on the money you borrowed doesn't cancel out the dividends you are earning.

For example, let's say that you had $5,000 to invest and you wanted to purchase shares priced at $20 a share with the dividend payout of $.50 per share. You could buy 250 shares and your annual dividend payout would be $125. However, with a margin of 20:1, which is a common ratio brokers offer in the stock market.

So, instead of having only $5,000 to invest, you suddenly have $100,000. In other words, you could buy 5,000 shares and your annual return would be $2,500 from dividends. However, nothing is free and margin lending does come with interest charges. This is why you have to make sure the interest you are paying on the money you borrowed doesn't completely offset any additional earnings you might make.

For example, if the interest is 1% per annum, that means you would be paying $950 to make a $2,500, which is not a bad deal at all. After all, you would have only made $125 without margin lending, whereas now you're making $1,550.

This is a simple calculation to show you the potential of this approach but you have to be certain you take into account all the fees and interest costs you pay, or you might end up losing money instead of making a profit.

Final Words About Investing in Nigeria

No matter where you intend to invest, dividend stocks are an ideal investment vehicle. This is especially true if you're taking a long-term view, which everyone should. As we've all seen, pension funds aren't completely reliable, so why put your financial future in someone else's hands when you can easily do a better job yourself?

Dividend stocks can provide excellent earning opportunities. As long as you do your due diligence properly, there is very little chance you will lose money. Even if the dividend yield is equivalent to the inflation rate, in the worse case you are still protecting your capital by ensuring it preserves its value, which is hard to do if you keep your money under the mattress. However, it's rare for a dividend yield to be quite that low.

Remember you have plenty of options, so make sure to do your research properly and you'll soon build up your wealth. There's nothing quite as satisfying as having a passive income stream you build up on your own and the financial freedom to do whatever you choose.

While investing in a country like Nigeria might seem highly exotic, the basic investment principles are the same for any stock market in the world. It probably is easier for many investors to penetrate the market because of the lower share prices, meaning you get started for a much smaller investment. This represents a great advantage because if you focus on dividend stocks, you can start off with a smaller investment and use the Nigerian stock market as a stepping-stone to build wealth and reinvest in more established stock markets across the world.

Since Nigeria is still considered an emerging market, the level of risk associated with an investment there can be considered somewhat higher but the returns usually reflect this. That is why you may also want to diversify your portfolio by purchasing stocks in well-established, stable companies, as well as in various countries. While there are plenty of options for you to look at in terms of Nigerian companies, you will find that the stocks that produce a good level of income while being stable are in the same sectors in anywhere in the world. In other words, you want to look at foods, beverages and tobacco sector, agriculture and the building materials sectors.

These are basically things people can't do without, no matter what the economy is doing.

Therefore, if you invest in the conglomerates or foods, beverages and tobacco companies you can be certain to see a good return on your investment for the long term because people will always need these services. It doesn't matter if there's another financial crisis tomorrow in the US, or anywhere for that matter, these companies will continue to perform because they provide vital services that people simply can't do without.

Of course, you should not limit yourself, but until you get to know the country and how its economy works, these are some safe bets to start with. Since we have been discussing investing in a foreign country, you should also take some time to get to know the local economy very well, along with any other factors that could influence it. These can include such things as politics, social issues and so on.

Remember, that these issues can actually be opportunities, because any form of social unrest will drive the price of stock down, allowing you to get great bargains and make a very nice profit when the market bounces back.

Again, the secret to successful investing in Nigerian stocks is to treat them as you would any other company shares. This means doing your due diligence, including closely analyzing company fundamentals and checking your facts.

If you are looking for a broker so you can invest in the stock market in Nigeria, your best option is to visit the Securities & Exchange Commission Nigeria website at www.sec.gov.ng, where a comprehensive list of registered market operators is available.

To obtain financial information on various companies, you can either visit their websites or contact them directly and ask for copies of their annual reports. In most cases, though, this information is freely and readily available online.

Some of the Nigerian Stock Brokers

http://www.afrinvest.com : Afrinvest west Africa limited

www.bglltd.com : BGL securities limited

http://www.cashcraft.com : Cash craft asset management limited

http://www.capitalassetsng.com : Capital Assets Nigeria Ltd

http://www.fslng.com/main.php : First stock brokers limited

http://www.gticapitalltd.com : GTI capital limited

http://www.vetiva.com : Vetiva capital management limited

http://www.zenithsecuritiesng.com : Zenith securities limited

http://www.bestworth-ltd.com : BestWorth Ltd

http://www.calyxsec.com : Calyx securities limited

http://signetng.com/?pg=home : Signet Investment&Securities Ltd

Some of the Nigerian Banks

http://www.firstbanknigeria.com

http://www.ubagroup.com

http://www.zenithbank.com

http://www.gtbank.com

Other Useful Resources

http://www.sec.gov.ng : securities and exchange commission

http://www.zenithbank.com/pricelist.cfm : Nigerian Daily stock updates
http://www.nigerianstockexchange.com

http://www.cashcraft.com : Click price list by sector for Daily Price List

 http://www.proshareng.com : Market updates and Analysis

With Dividend Stocks In the Nigerian Stock Market

http://www.cscsnigerialtd.com : (CSCS) Limited is a subsidiary of The Nigerian Stock Exchange (NSE) as well as the Clearing House of the Nigerian Stock Market.

http://www.247BroadStreet.com: The only Nigerian website that teaches you a simple, step-by-step strategy that can help you profit in the Nigerian stock market.

Note: Your capital is at risk when you invest in shares - you can lose some or all of your money, so never risk more than you can afford to lose. Always seek professional advice if you are unsure about the suitability of any investment. Past performance is not a reliable indicator of future results.

Have You Read?

The Guide to Investing in the Nigerian Stock Market. This is the neatest, concise, clear guide to Investing in the Nigerian stock market. This is a must have book.

www.ingramcontent.com/pod-product-compliance
Lightning Source LLC
Chambersburg PA
CBHW051344170526
45166CB00002B/954